The Gecko Without an Echo

Author

Cheryl Denise Bannerman

Illustrator

Anushka Bansal

© 2024 Cheryl Denise Bannerman. All rights reserved.

Print paperback format: ISBN 979-8985401585

eBook: ISBN 979-8985401530

No part of this book may be reproduced, stored in a retrieval system, or transmitted by any means without the written permission of the author.

This is a work of fiction. All the characters, names, incidents, organizations, and dialogue in this novel are either the products of the author's imagination or are used fictitiously.

Dedicated to my daughter.

On a cold and cloudy day
In a tree by the bay,

There lived a gecko named Earl
With his friend Tim, the squirrel.

Tim and Earl were quite the pair,
They traveled together everywhere.

From deep in the valley below
To the highest peak they'd go,

And most days, happiness filled the air
But on this particular day, Earl was in despair.

For when Earl shouted his name to the sky so high
Mother Nature had no reply.

Thinking her rudeness was by choice
Earl thought his echo had no voice.

"But I heard you, my friend," said Tim with a sigh
Even when there is no reply.

"Who ever heard of a gecko with no echo? It's supposed to follow you wherever you go!"

I've called "hello" from high to low
And called out every language I know.

There's hola, bonjour, and guten tag too,
I do not know what else to do.

Tim joined his friend in summoning the echo
And they both tried calling from high and low.

Then one sunny day by the glistening bay
They came across a cave on the way to play.

They ventured inside and the sun seemed to fade,
While they followed the path that another had laid.

Then around the bend they found a treasure,
A secret that was beyond measure.

It was a pond in the cave before their eyes
With a ceiling so high that a plane could fly,

Surrounded by sand as white as snow
And rippling water with the bluest glow.

Just then Earl had the fanciest thought
He stood up tall to speak, as he was taught.

Just then they heard a voice of a boy "Helloooo!" filled the cave and they jumped with joy.

Tim and Earl were filled with glee "My voice! It has come right back to me!"

"I'm no longer a gecko with no echo, you see. Mother Nature is not mad at me!"

Tim said, "I understand your joy, don't get me wrong. But, actually, your voice was heard all along."

By the birds and the bees, and all of the trees,
By the bears, and the deer, and even the geese.

But most important of all, it was heard by me
Your friend for life, by the bay, in our tree.

So, even when you think you are not heard
Just use your voice and don't be scared.

TIM AND EARL FRIENDS FOREVER

Whether happy or sad, those who call you friend
Will listen and love you to the very end.

About the Author

Cheryl Denise Bannerman is an award-winning, multi-genre author of eight published works of fiction – from murder mysteries to a recent children's book about friendship.

She is the winner of the 2018 Book Excellence Award for her book of poetry, *Words Never Spoken*, and winner of the Best Books Awards in the category of African American fiction in 2020 for *Black Child to Black Woman.* She is also a Semi-Finalist in the MLC Audiobook Awards with a 2020 IMDb Nomination for Book 1 of the Anna Romano Mystery Series, *Cats, Cannolis, and a Curious Kidnapping*.

The author draws her inspiration from life experiences, observations, and lessons. Her goal in life is to keep writing and continue helping victims of Domestic Abuse/Violence, Grief and ANON family groups, and Corporate Health and Wellness groups, to heal through words — encouraging them to 'write the pain' via journaling, and expressing themselves through short stories, songs, and poetry.

When she is not working from her home office on her virtual Training and Development business, she is at the beach watching the waves and weaving the words together for her next novel.

Check out some of her other works of fiction at www.bannermanbooks.com.

www.ingramcontent.com/pod-product-compliance
Ingram Content Group UK Ltd.
Pitfield, Milton Keynes, MK11 3LW, UK
UKHW060216240426
12048UKWH00030BB/1699